MW01008462

✦ COUNTDOWN TO SPACE ✦
✦
✦   ✦
✦

CHRISTA McAULIFFE
A Space Biography

Laura S. Jeffrey

Series Advisor:
John E. McLeaish
Chief, Public Information Office, retired,
NASA Johnson Space Center

Enslow Publishers, Inc.

40 Industrial Road	PO Box 38
Box 398	Aldershot
Berkeley Heights, NJ 07922	Hants GU12 6BP
USA	UK

http://www.enslow.com

*The publisher is extremely grateful to Grace Corrigan,
mother of Christa McAuliffe, for generously offering some
of her family photographs for use in this book.*

Library of Congress Cataloging-in-Publication Data

Jeffrey, Laura S.
    Christa McAuliffe: a space biography / Laura S. Jeffrey.
        p. cm. — (Countdown to space)
    Includes bibliographical references and index.
    Summary: A biography of the school teacher turned astronaut whose life was
tragically ended when the space shuttle Challenger exploded just after liftoff.
    ISBN-10: 0-89490-976-2
    1. McAuliffe, Christa, 1948–1986—Biography—Juvenile literature.
2. Astronauts—United States—Biography—Juvenile literature 3. Teachers—
New Hampshire—Biography—Juvenile literature. 4. Challenger (Spacecraft)—
Juvenile literature. [1. McAuliffe, Christa, 1948–1986. 2. Astronauts.
3. Teachers. 4. Challenger (Spacecraft)—Accidents. 5. Women—Biography.]
    I. Title. II. Series.
    TL789.85.M33J44   1998
    629.4'0092—dc21
    [B]   97-22114
                                                  CIP
                                                  AC
ISBN-13: 978-0-89490-976-4

Printed in the United States of America

10 9 8 7 6

Illustration Credits: Courtesy of Grace Corrigan, pp. 13, 14, 15, 17, 18, 31,
38; National Aeronautics and Space Administration (NASA), pp. 4, 7, 8, 10,
21, 22, 24, 27, 28, 33, 35, 36.

Cover Illustration: National Aeronautics and Space Administration
(NASA) (foreground); Raghvendra Sahai and John Trauger (JPL), the
WFPC2 science team, NASA, and AURA/STSCI (background).

CONTENTS

Christa McAuliffe, shown here at the Kennedy Space Center during the launching of a Challenger *flight in 1985, was chosen to be the country's first citizen to travel aboard the space shuttle.*

Moment of Truth

The people who had gathered at the Kennedy Space Center in Florida on September 29, 1988, were tense and anxious. They were about to witness the launching of the space shuttle *Discovery*. This would be the twenty-sixth time that the National Aeronautics and Space Administration (NASA) had conducted a shuttle launch.

Almost all of the previous shuttle launches had been successful. Astronauts soared into space, performed experiments, and then returned triumphantly to Earth. However, something had gone terribly wrong during the twenty-fifth launching more than two years before. On January 28, 1986, the space shuttle *Challenger* blasted into space. Among those on board was a person who had become very familiar to Americans. Her name was

Christa McAuliffe. She was not an astronaut but a teacher. McAuliffe had been chosen among thousands of educators to become the first teacher in space. Her enthusiasm, energy, and sense of adventure made her a natural to assume this historic position.

President Ronald Reagan and NASA officials had hoped that including an ordinary American on a shuttle flight would spark public enthusiasm in the space program. Space travel had become so routine that many Americans had lost interest in it.

McAuliffe, in turn, wished to reveal the wonders of space exploration to schoolchildren. She planned to keep a diary of her experiences and to conduct lessons from space. After returning to Earth, she wanted to visit schools around the country to talk about her incredible journey. Finally, she planned to return to her own classroom in New Hampshire to continue her teaching career. All of those hopes and dreams, however, had disappeared on that bitter cold January day.

At first, the *Challenger* launch seemed routine. "Have a good mission," launch director Gene Thomas told the crew members shortly before liftoff. "Thanks a bunch," replied commander Francis "Dick" Scobee. "We'll see you when we get back."[1] Besides McAuliffe and Scobee, the other astronauts on the shuttle were Michael Smith, Ellison Onizuka, Judith Resnik, Ronald McNair, and Gregory Jarvis.

At 11:38 A.M., the *Challenger* blasted into space. An

The seven crewmates of the space shuttle Challenger: (from left to right, front row) Mike Smith, Dick Scobee, Ron McNair; (back row) Ellison Onizuka, Christa McAuliffe, Gregory Jarvis, and Judith Resnik.

external fuel tank was on the bottom side of the shuttle's orbiter. This large, orange tank contained more than 500,000 gallons of fuel. A solid rocket booster was on each side of the fuel tank.

As the shuttle headed high into the sky, the crowd of spectators cheered. Among those watching were McAuliffe's parents, siblings, husband, and two young children. Their joy was short-lived, however. After only seventy-three seconds in the air, the shuttle exploded. It broke apart and fell back to Earth. All of the crew members were killed.

Many in the crowd were confused. They continued

to stare into the sky. Soon their confusion turned into the realization that something terrible had happened. McAuliffe's sister screamed. "I heard sobs as fragments [of the spacecraft] tumbled out of the reddish brown smoke and plummeted into the ocean," McAuliffe's mother, Grace Corrigan, later recalled. "I wanted desperately to believe things would be okay. But then the voice of an announcer declared there had been 'a major malfunction.' Ed [McAuliffe's father] turned to me and said, 'She's gone.'"[2]

Cheryl McNair, who was married to astronaut

After only seventy-three seconds in the air, the Challenger *exploded.*

Ronald McNair, remembered, "I watched the liftoff, and the shuttle went straight up. It turned down. I knew something was *wrong.*"[3]

Astronaut Michael Smith's young daughter was also aware that something terrible had happened. She screamed for her father. "Daddy! I want you, Daddy!" she cried. "You always promised nothing would happen!"[4]

Across the country, schoolchildren watched the tragedy unfold on television sets in their classrooms. The image of the fiery explosion in the clear blue sky was replayed time and again as America mourned the heroic crew.

The space shuttle program shut down. There were no launches for more than two years. NASA workers spent that time designing and building a new, safer shuttle. Finally, in September 1988, the day had come for Americans to return to space. The experienced astronauts onboard had trained longer than any other shuttle crew in history.

Surely nothing would go wrong with the *Discovery* launch. Still, people were worried. Would another tragedy occur, killing more people and possibly shutting down the space program forever?

Thankfully, that did not happen. The *Discovery* lifted off into space at about 11:30 A.M. Around the world, there were cheers and tears. "Wow!" exclaimed NASA administrator James Fletcher shortly after liftoff. "That was really something." Said one of the astronauts, "We sure appreciate you all gettin' us up into orbit where we should be."[5]

The *Discovery* spent several days in space. On their last full day of the mission, they read a memorial message in honor of the seven who had died aboard *Challenger.* "Dear friends," the message said, "we have resumed the journey that we promised to continue for you. Your spirit and your dreams are still alive in our hearts."[6]

More than fifty launches have occurred since *Discovery*'s voyage in 1988. All of them have been successful. Yet while public confidence in the space program had been restored, memories of the *Challenger* disaster remained vivid.

The image of Christa McAuliffe was particularly haunting. Most of the others who died in the tragedy were seasoned pros, accustomed to

Christa McAuliffe, center, was not afraid to face the challenge of venturing into space. Here, she and backup teacher Barbara Morgan (right) take a break from shuttle training at the Johnson Space Center.

the dangers of their job. McAuliffe, on the other hand, was seen as a neighbor, a friend. Through television, newspaper, and magazine reports leading up to the launch, many Americans felt as though they had really come to know her. "Every mission has its hazards," astronaut Ellison Onizuka once said. "It requires a lot of training and hundreds of people working together on the ground to make sure it's not a catastrophe. There are still a lot of questions about the shuttle, and we need to make sure it's as safe as possible before we start flying too many civilians."[7]

McAuliffe, however, was confident. "I don't see it as a dangerous thing to do," she once said. Then she added, "Well, I suppose it is, with all those rockets and fuel tanks. But if I saw it as a big risk, I'd feel differently."[8]

Who was this woman who embarked on that fateful trip, the one she once called "the ultimate field trip"?[9] Christa McAuliffe was a daughter, a wife, and a mother. She had a keen sense of adventure and believed in living life to its fullest. She was greatly interested in space and wanted others to share her excitement and wonderment. She was simply an ordinary person, called on to do an extraordinary thing.

Growing Up

From the time she was a young girl, Christa McAuliffe was energetic and enthusiastic. She was born Sharon Christa Corrigan on September 2, 1948, in Boston, Massachusetts. Her parents, Ed and Grace Corrigan, simply called her Christa.

Ed Corrigan was a college student when Christa was a baby, so the family did not start out with much money. Things improved after he graduated from college. He earned a degree in business administration.

In 1954, when Christa was seven, she and her parents and her two younger brothers moved to Framingham, Massachusetts. The family grew. Ed and Grace Corrigan had two more girls. Their oldest child proved to be a good big sister. Christa baby-sat her siblings. She also taught her two sisters how to sew and knit.

Throughout her childhood, Christa was very active. She took voice, dance, piano, and guitar lessons. She performed in school plays. She also joined the Girl Scouts. This was an activity that Christa would be involved with for the rest of her life.

In 1958, when Christa was ten years old, President Dwight D. Eisenhower established the National Aeronautics and Space Administration. Three years later, President John F. Kennedy announced that Americans would soon land on the Moon. Christa was interested in the space program. She had no idea, however, that one day she would be a part of it.

As a teenager, Christa continued to lead a busy life. She entered Marian High School, a Catholic school, and played basketball and softball. She volunteered to help others through her church. On top of all this, she worked part-time. Some

Christa Corrigan grew up in Massachusetts.

As a teenager, Christa enjoyed sports, scouts, church, and school.

of her jobs were teaching children to swim and clerking at a dry cleaners. "Her face was very alive, very interested," recalled a former teacher. "You could tell by looking at her that she was excited about everything life held before her."[1]

Christa also found time to watch television. "I know I loved *Star Trek* when I was in high school," she once said. "I thought that it was just a neat idea that someday there would be people living on spaceships."[2]

On the first day of her sophomore year, Christa met a new boy in class. His name was Steve McAuliffe. Christa and Steve became friends and dated throughout high school. By the time the couple graduated in 1966, they had their futures planned. Steve wanted to be a lawyer. He decided to attend Virginia Military Institute for his undergraduate degree. Christa wanted to be a history teacher. She attended Framingham State College in Massachusetts and lived at home. On many weekends, she drove to Virginia to visit Steve.

While Christa was in college, the United States space program was in high gear. Testing on manned flights had begun in May 1961. In January 1967, a fire broke out in the *Apollo 1* command module during a flight simulation. The three astronauts aboard—Virgil "Gus" Grissom, Edward H. White, and Roger B. Chaffee—were killed. There was better news two years later when Neil Armstrong and Edwin "Buzz" Aldrin actually walked on the Moon.

In 1970, Christa and Steve graduated from their colleges. Deeply in love, they were married that August. The newlyweds moved to Maryland. Steve McAuliffe attended law school at Georgetown University in nearby Washington, D.C. His wife began her teaching career at Benjamin Foulois Junior High School in Morningside, Maryland. After a year, she transferred

In August 1970, Christa Corrigan and Steve McAuliffe were married.

to Thomas Johnson Middle School in Bowie, Maryland. There she taught English, American history, and civics. McAuliffe brought alive the lessons she taught. She often took her history students on field trips to historic areas such as Williamsburg, Virginia. Her civics classes visited local courts and prisons.

In September 1976, the couple's first child, Scott, was born. Christa McAuliffe continued to teach. She also became involved in school administration. She was leader of the faculty advisory committee. She stepped in as the temporary principal when the full-time principal was out for several months with an illness. McAuliffe decided to earn a degree in school administration. Studying at nights and on weekends, she earned her master's degree from Bowie State College in 1978.

During the 1970s, NASA began to develop a space shuttle. Unlike previous spacecraft, the shuttle was reusable. Also, the shuttle enabled astronauts to conduct experiments to learn more about space travel in general. In 1977, America's first space shuttle, the *Enterprise*, flew atop a jet in a test. At 24,000 feet above Earth, it separated from the jet and glided to a landing. It continued to make such test flights in 1978. That same year, Steve McAuliffe received a job offer in New Hampshire. Always ready for a new adventure, the McAuliffes moved. They settled in the state capital, a small town called Concord. Steve McAuliffe was a lawyer in the attorney general's office. Later, he became a lawyer in a private practice.

Christa McAuliffe, meanwhile, taught English and history at Rundlett Junior High School. She took a short break to give birth to the couple's second child, Caroline, in August 1979. Two months after Caroline's birth, McAuliffe returned to teaching. She worked at a high school called Bow Memorial School. When a position as assistant principal became available, McAuliffe applied. She was told that she did not get the job because the school was not ready for a woman to be in charge.[3]

Disappointed, McAuliffe looked for other teaching

The arrival of Caroline McAuliffe was a happy occasion for the family. Pictured with Christa are her grandmother, holding baby Caroline, and her mother.

opportunities. She learned that Concord High School, only a few blocks from her home, had an opening. She started working there in 1982.

At Concord, McAuliffe created a course called The American Woman. It focused on ordinary people's views of American history. "One of my problems in teaching history is that ordinary people are not given a lot of attention," she once said. "You learn dates, you learn about generals and presidents and how many bodies

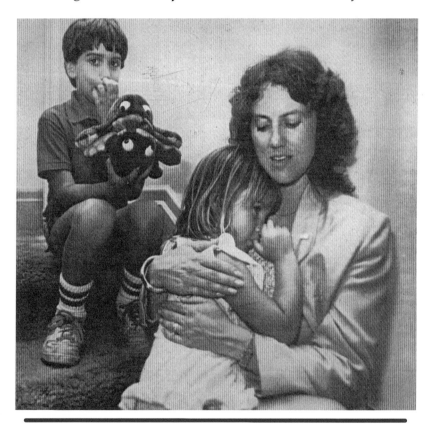

Christa is shown with two of her biggest fans—daughter, Caroline, and son, Scott.

there were in the war, but you don't find out what happened to individual[s]."[4]

McAuliffe continued to take her students on field trips. She was very popular with her pupils, mainly because she encouraged them to follow their dreams. "Any dream can come true if you have the courage to work at it," she often told them.[5]

As a teacher, McAuliffe had a special way of making her students feel comfortable. "I never saw a teacher hold a class's attention the way she did, even with the problem kids," a former student recalled. "Right from the first day . . . she got us to memorize every student's name. I think that was how she got us to start thinking and caring about each other."[6]

When she was not teaching, McAuliffe led a Girl Scout troop. She taught religious education at her church, performed in community theater, jogged, and played volleyball and tennis. She also was a devoted mom to Scott and Caroline.

McAuliffe's life was full and happy. It did not seem as though she needed, or even had time for, anything else. In August 1984, however, she heard an intriguing news report over her car radio. NASA was looking for a teacher to become the first "ordinary" person in space.

3

Making the Grade

"I'm directing NASA to begin a search in all our elementary and secondary schools," President Reagan announced, "and to choose as the first citizen passenger in our space program, one of America's finest, a teacher."[1]

For some time before Reagan's announcement, NASA had been receiving thousands of letters from people who wanted to take a ride on the space shuttle. The space agency formed a committee to determine if this was a safe thing to do. Following the committee's recommendations, NASA decided to choose at least two people to ride on shuttle flights in 1986. More people would be chosen for flights in subsequent years. As its first participant, NASA recommended choosing a teacher. The agency thought this would be a good way to spark young people's interest in the space program.

"We're not looking for Superman," a NASA spokesman said. "We're looking for the person who can do the best job of describing his or her experiences on the shuttle to the most people on Earth."[2]

Christa McAuliffe was excited about the announcement. She thought that sending a teacher into space would spark interest not only in the space program but also in public schools. Still, if she were chosen, she would have to spend a lot of time away from her family. She was not even sure she was qualified for space travel. What should she do? "Go for it!" her husband replied.[3]

A few months later, McAuliffe picked up a request form for an application. A thick application packet arrived in the mail, but McAuliffe put it aside. She did not turn in her application until the day it was due, February 1, 1985. "I did a lot of things I tell you

President Reagan directed NASA to select a teacher to become America's first citizen passenger aboard the space shuttle.

kids not to do," she later told her students. "I waited till the absolute last minute."[4]

McAuliffe was one of more than eleven thousand teachers who applied. NASA decided to choose two finalists from each state. These finalists would then travel to Washington, D.C., for personal interviews and medical exams. In April 1985, McAuliffe learned that she was one of New Hampshire's two finalists.

The enthusiastic teacher crammed for her interview as though she were studying for final exams. All of the teachers were required to submit a videotape of themselves speaking so that the judges could become familiar with them. McAuliffe asked friends for makeup and clothing tips. She also practiced several times on camera before making the tape.

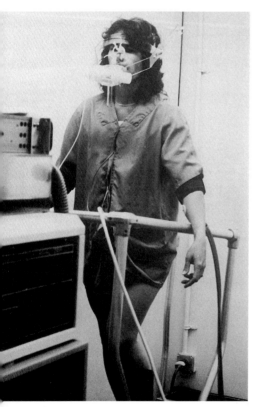

The finalists also had to describe a project they would complete during their space mission. Some teachers proposed complex scientific

As a finalist in The Teacher in Space Project, Christa McAuliffe took physical tests. Here, she runs on a treadmill so that her body's responses can be recorded.

experiments. McAuliffe's idea, however, was simple yet profound. She would keep a journal of her experiences. This would be a good way to stay busy in space, she reasoned. It would help her remember everything so that she could share her experiences once she returned.

The morning that McAuliffe returned home to New Hampshire, she was awakened by a telephone call. She had been chosen as one of the ten finalists. Leaving her family once again, McAuliffe traveled to the Johnson Space Center in Houston, Texas. She and the nine other finalists took more physical tests as well as psychological tests. They also underwent space simulations and met again with the judges. "All ten teachers were outstanding people," one judge later said. "But some of them concentrated too much on how wonderful it would be to fly in the space shuttle, rather than on how they would use the experience to get teachers excited about the space program. Christa was the one who most clearly understood what we had in mind."[5]

The judges took only twenty minutes to decide on their pick: Christa McAuliffe. They also chose an alternate, Barbara Morgan. She was a second-grade teacher from McCall, Idaho.

The finalists were called back to Washington, D.C., in July 1985. None of them knew who had been chosen. On July 19, Vice President George Bush held a press conference at the White House. Reporters and

As Department of Education Director William Bennett and Vice President George Bush look on, McAuliffe accepts being selected as NASA's first teacher in space.

photographers listened as Bush announced that Christa McAuliffe would be the first ordinary American in space. Then the Vice President presented McAuliffe with a statue. It depicted a teacher reaching toward the sky.

McAuliffe held back tears as she gave a short speech. Afterward, she was swamped by reporters. "I'm still kind of floating," she said when she was asked how she felt. "I don't know when I'll come down to Earth."[6]

McAuliffe became an instant celebrity in her hometown. She was the guest of honor in a parade on August 6, 1985, when Concord celebrated Christa

McAuliffe Day. Soon her celebrity spread nationwide. McAuliffe attended a state dinner at the White House and sat next to President Reagan. She appeared on television shows such as *The MacNeil/Lehrer News Hour* and *The Tonight Show*. Americans were struck by how sincere and modest she was. She said she was not the best teacher, but definitely one of the luckiest.

McAuliffe also was very enthusiastic. "It's going to be a wonderful ride," she said. "But the thought that I'm going to bring this back to people on all different levels and maybe make them proud of the program and want to learn more about it—now, that's a really exciting thing for a teacher."[7]

She also said, "You know, people come up to me and say, 'I really admire you but I wouldn't want to do it.' I can't understand that. If you had a chance, wouldn't *you* want to do it?"[8]

The interviews and television appearances were fun for McAuliffe, but there was serious work to be done. As one NASA official said, "It's not like [McAuliffe] puts on a suit and off she goes. She has to pass tests or she won't fly."[9] So once again, McAuliffe said good-bye to her husband and two children. She was off to Houston, Texas. She spent the next four months training for her historic flight. She never could have imagined they would be the last four months of her life.

4

Smoke in the Sky

Christa McAuliffe settled into a furnished apartment near the Johnson Space Center. This would be the teacher's home for several months while she prepared to ride aboard the space shuttle *Challenger*. McAuliffe learned how the shuttle worked. She learned how to eat, sleep, and work in space. She watched mock drills on emergency landings and other procedures.

McAuliffe wrote weekly to the Concord High School newspaper, describing her activities. She also planned and practiced the lessons she would give aboard the shuttle via television broadcasts. One lesson was a field trip through the spacecraft. Another was a discussion of the various uses of the shuttle. After a full day of work, McAuliffe would often spend several more hours reading books to prepare for the next day's lessons. Her days were full but rewarding.

The other crew members were an impressive group. Dick Scobee was commander of the *Challenger*. He was a former Air Force test pilot who had been in space before. Mike Smith, the shuttle pilot, was also a former test pilot. This would be his first spaceflight. Ron McNair, a mission specialist, had been the second African American to travel in space, after Guion Bluford in 1983. Mission specialist Ellison Onizuka also had made another shuttle trip. He was the first Japanese American in space. Mission specialist Judith Resnik had

In her second week of training, McAuliffe familiarized herself with camera equipment that would be used on the shuttle.

McAuliffe descends from a mockup of the shuttle using a sky-genie device during an emergency training session at the Johnson Space Center.

been the second American woman in space, after Sally Ride in 1983. Payload specialist Gregory Jarvis was a civilian engineer. He had helped design the satellite that was scheduled to be launched from the *Challenger*. Jarvis had been bumped from two earlier shuttle flights to make room for congressmen who had flown with the crews. He was very excited that it was finally his turn. "If they sold tickets, I'd be the first to buy one," he once said.[1]

At first, McAuliffe was concerned about how the astronauts would react to having a rookie on board. But the teacher quickly won them over with her willingness to learn and work hard. They also were impressed with how much interest she had sparked in the space program. As Scobee told her, "Missions keep going up every month, but the teacher in space is unique. *You're the reason we'll be remembered.*"[2]

McAuliffe developed warm relationships with her

colleagues. One time, Ellison Onizuka was showing her around the shuttle. "If you can read, you'll probably stay out of trouble," he joked. The teacher joked back, "I won't make any rash promises."[3]

McAuliffe also became close friends with Barbara Morgan, the teacher alternate. Morgan trained in Houston with McAuliffe and the astronauts. If anything happened to McAuliffe before the shuttle flight, Morgan would take her place. The two teachers often went jogging or simply relaxed after a hard day of training.

While McAuliffe was busy in Houston, Steve McAuliffe ran the household in Concord, New Hampshire. He cheerfully referred to himself as a "space husband"[4] and took good care of Scott and Caroline. Still, Christa McAuliffe missed her children. She worried about the impact of her absence. Scott and Caroline "understand what's going on," she said, "but I don't know whether they totally appreciate it right now."[5] She kept in touch through phone calls and occasional visits, but the separation was hard for McAuliffe.

She also missed the pupils at Concord High. "I miss my students telling me about their dates," she said.[6] She worried that her absence would affect their studies. "Students tell me, 'I've been waiting three years to take your course, and now you're not there,'" she added.[7]

Nonetheless, McAuliffe recognized that her personal sacrifices were worth the effort. She once said,

When I talk to my [students], I liken what I'm going

to do to the women who pioneered the West. . . . They described things in vivid detail, in word pictures. They were concerned with daily tasks and the interaction between people. . . . I'll be able to take the time to report on feelings and emotions; how it is to live in a close environment with people you don't really know; housekeeping; weightlessness . . . Eating! Kids may not relate to satellites, but they can relate to breakfast, lunch and dinner.[8]

The *Challenger* launch was originally scheduled for January 23, 1986, at the Kennedy Space Center in Florida. The launch date was changed several times because of bad weather and other problems. One time, the astronauts were actually strapped into their seats in the shuttle for five hours before the mission was postponed.

Some officials were becoming frustrated with the delays. They also were worried. A full schedule of shuttle flights was planned for 1986, with many missions to accomplish. If more delays occurred, some important deadlines would be missed.

Meanwhile, more than fifteen thousand guests had arrived at the Kennedy Space Center to watch the historic launch. Scott McAuliffe's entire third-grade class had come from New Hampshire. Other students in New Hampshire and other states would watch the launch live via television sets in their schools. McAuliffe's mother, father, husband, children, siblings, and college friends were in the crowd. They were so

One week prior to the Challenger *launch, Christa spent some time with her mom, Grace Corrigan, in Cape Canaveral.*

excited to watch Christa McAuliffe achieve the impressive goal she had set.

Early on the morning of January 28, 1986, McAuliffe and the astronauts took their places on the *Challenger*. Would today finally be launch day? It was below freezing that morning, only 27 degrees Fahrenheit. The shuttle had never before been launched in such cold weather. In fact, NASA officials had stayed up late the night before talking about another launch delay. They discussed it again on the morning of the 28th. Some engineers had recommended against the launch. They were worried that rubber seals on the rockets, called

O-rings, would weaken in cold weather and allow gas to escape. The results would be disastrous.

In the end, however, the engineers were overruled. NASA gave the go-ahead for the launch. While McAuliffe and the others waited inside the shuttle, their family members were taken to a special viewing area on top of a NASA building. Finally, at 11:15 A.M., the astronauts were told that the launch was a go. "All right!" said Scobee. "That's great."[9]

At 11:38 A.M., the shuttle's rockets ignited and the spacecraft blasted off. The crowd cheered as they looked toward the sky. Less than two minutes later, however, they knew something was terribly wrong. The shuttle, nine miles up in the air, had exploded. As it fell back to Earth, it left a huge cloud of smoke in the sky. The crew's last known words were uttered by pilot Mike Smith just before the explosion. "Uhh . . . oh!" he said.[10]

NASA officials quickly moved the astronauts' family members into a waiting area inside the building. Grace Corrigan, Christa's mother, began to get very upset. "The craft has exploded, the craft has exploded," she chanted over and over. Ellison Onizuka's wife fainted. As she fell near the wall, she brushed against the light switch, plunging the room into darkness. After about fifteen minutes, another NASA official arrived. "We don't know all the details, but it looks like there has been an explosion," he said gravely. "I don't believe there is any hope for the crew."[11]

Ice formation on the shuttle proved to be the reason for the Challenger *explosion.*

The White House was notified immediately. Aide Patrick Buchanan rushed into the Oval Office, where President Reagan was working, to tell him the news. "Sir, the shuttle's blown up," he said. The President looked shocked and upset. "Isn't that the one with the teacher on it?" he asked.[12]

The teacher. The *Challenger*. Christa McAuliffe and the other brave Americans aboard the space shuttle were dead. It seemed as if the entire nation felt tremendous sorrow. That sorrow quickly turned into outrage, however. The accident had been avoidable.

5

Remembering
the Heroes

Three days after the terrible accident, a memorial service was held at the Johnson Space Center in Texas. President and Mrs. Reagan flew from Washington, D.C., to address the *Challenger* crew's loved ones. During the memorial, Mrs. Reagan hugged Grace Corrigan, Christa McAuliffe's mother. "In one cruel moment, our exhilaration turned to horror," President Reagan said.[1]

The McAuliffe family held a funeral for Christa on February 3, 1986, in Concord, New Hampshire. Grace and Ed Corrigan moved there temporarily to take care of their confused and sad grandchildren. They also helped Steve McAuliffe sort through cards and letters from people all over the world.

"Tears have flowed in my city for days," said Mike

Pride, editor of the *Monitor* newspaper in Concord. "It is not a myth to say that everyone in town knew Christa. She was easy to meet, easy to talk to. Even those who never had the chance [to meet her] felt as though they had."[2]

President Reagan called a panel together to investigate why the *Challenger* had exploded. William Rogers, a former secretary of state, led the thirteen-member panel. Members included Sally Ride, the first American woman in space, and Neil Armstrong, the first human to walk on the Moon.

The panel was called the Rogers Commission. Its members studied the shuttle debris. They listened to testimony from NASA officials, rocket engineers, and others who worked on the space program. In June 1986, the commission released a report. It said that a rubber

The remains of the Challenger *crew were moved from the Kennedy Space Center to the Dover Air Force Base in Delaware.*

pressure seal known as an O-ring had failed because of the cold weather and wind. This seal was located on the right solid rocket booster. Flaming gas from this leaking joint broke the connection between the rocket booster and the rest of the space shuttle. As the booster broke off, it tore a hole in the external fuel tank. The tank contained thousands of gallons of liquid hydrogen and oxygen. It exploded, and the shuttle broke apart.[3] The compartment carrying McAuliffe and the other astronauts remained intact, however. It fell to the Atlantic Ocean with the astronauts strapped helplessly inside.[4]

Wreckage from the Challenger *shuttle was retrieved from the Atlantic Ocean by a flotilla of U.S. Coast Guard and U.S. Navy vessels.*

In fact, the compartment was found in the ocean about a month after the accident. "It was a twisted-up mess," recalled Cheryl McNair, widow of astronaut Ron McNair. "I couldn't help thinking about what it must have been like to be onboard."[5]

The Rogers Commission report also said that NASA officials had ignored warnings from some engineers that the shuttle was unsafe in cold weather. Some people believed that the space agency felt a lot of pressure to launch. A former NASA safety director noted,

> There was social pressure: they had thousands of school kids watching for the first school lesson from space. There was media pressure: they feared that if they didn't launch, the press would unfavorably report more delays. And there was commercial pressure: the [European launcher] was putting objects in space at much lower cost. . . . The pressures were subtle, but they acted upon them.[6]

After the report was released, some officials who had ignored the engineers' warnings lost their jobs. Rules were set up to force supervisors to listen to safety warnings. Also, the shuttle was almost completely redesigned. It included a crew-escape system and a fire-detection system for the external fuel tank. Stronger seals were placed on the solid rocket boosters. Hatches were reworked so that they could be opened from inside the shuttle. Also, parachutes and personal oxygen supplies became standard equipment for astronauts.

Even with these changes, NASA officials warned that

space travel remained risky. They made no plans to resume the citizen-in-space program. "Somewhere in the future of our country I think we are going to have another accident," said NASA associate administrator Richard Truly after the *Discovery* launch. "It's inevitable."[7]

Steve McAuliffe became a federal judge and is married to another teacher. In time, the pain of losing Christa subsided. Knowing that Christa had touched so many lives helped her family heal. The special teacher was honored in many ways. Framingham State College, Christa McAuliffe's alma mater, established the Christa Corrigan McAuliffe Center for Education and Teaching Excellence. The center awards scholarships to worthy students.

In another memorial, seven trees—one for each crew member—were planted in a park near the McAuliffe home in New Hampshire. An elementary school in Kansas was named after McAuliffe. Also, the Christa

A bronze statue of Christa McAuliffe was made from melted pennies that were collected from students in memory of the unforgettable teacher. The sculpture was dedicated during a garden ceremony in West Virginia.

McAuliffe Planetarium opened at the New Hampshire Technical Institute in Concord.

The families of McAuliffe and the other crew members wanted to make their own memorial. They established the Challenger Center for Space Science Education in Alexandria, Virginia. The center has programs at twenty-five sites across the United States and Canada. In 1996, about 250,000 middle-school students participated in simulated spaceflights.[8]

As important as the physical reminders were personal testimonies. Micaela Mejia was one example. Mejia lived across the street from the McAuliffes and often baby-sat Caroline and Scott. She once thought about becoming a journalist, but then decided to follow McAuliffe into teaching. Mejia became a fourth-grade teacher in Virginia. "The more I talked about her, the more I understood how incredible she was, how what teachers do is so incredible," Mejia said. "It's doing something that will make a difference in people's lives."[9]

In January 1996, Americans marked the tenth anniversary of the *Challenger* explosion. In an interview, Grace Corrigan was asked why her daughter became so beloved, even though she was in the spotlight for such a short period of time.

"I think it's because she made us feel good about ourselves," Corrigan replied. "She proved that an ordinary person could accomplish extraordinary things. The trick is that you must try."[10]

CHRONOLOGY

1948—Sharon Christa Corrigan born on September 2 in Boston, Massachusetts.

1954—Moved with her family to Framingham, Massachusetts.

1958—President Dwight D. Eisenhower established the National Aeronautics and Space Administration.

1961—NASA began testing on manned spaceflights.

1966—Christa graduated from Marian High School; entered Framingham State College.

1967—Three astronauts aboard *Apollo 1* were killed in a fire during a flight simulation.

1968—Astronauts aboard *Apollo 8* made the first manned flight around the Moon.

1969—*Apollo 11* astronauts Neil Armstrong and Edwin "Buzz" Aldrin became the first humans to walk on the Moon.

1970—Christa graduated from Framingham State College; married Steve McAuliffe; began her teaching career.

1976—Son Scott was born.

1977—America's first space shuttle, the *Enterprise*, made test flights atop a jet.

1978—Earned a master's degree in school administration from Bowie State College; moved with husband and son to Concord, New Hampshire.

1979—Daughter Caroline was born.

1982—Began teaching at Concord High School.

1985—Applied to become the first teacher in space in February; named one of the finalists in April; named the first teacher in space in July; Christa McAuliffe Day declared in Concord, New Hampshire, on August 6.

1986—Space shuttle *Challenger* exploded seventy-three seconds after liftoff on January 28, killing Christa McAuliffe and six others; memorial held at the Johnson Space Center in Texas on January 31; Christa McAuliffe buried in Concord, New Hampshire, on February 3; Rogers Commission released its report on the explosion in June.

1988—Shuttle returned to space as *Discovery* blasted off on September 29.

1996—Tenth anniversary of *Challenger* explosion was marked.

CHAPTER NOTES

Chapter 1

1. Robert T. Hohler, *"I Touch the Future . . .": The Story of Christa McAuliffe* (New York: Random House, 1986), p. 254.

2. Grace Corrigan, as told to Donna Elizabeth Boetig, "The Whole World Loved My Daughter," *McCall's*, January 1996, p. 62.

3. Kathryn Casey, "Remembering the Challenger," *Ladies' Home Journal*, January 1996, p. 100.

4. Ibid., p. 149.

5. Geoffrey Cowley, "Special Report," *Newsweek*, October 10, 1988, p. 24.

6. Barbara Embury, *The Dream Is Alive: A Flight of Discovery Aboard the Space Shuttle* (New York: Harper & Row Publishers, 1990), p. 10.

7. Hohler, p. 209.

8. Grace George Corrigan, *A Journal for Christa: Christa McAuliffe, Teacher in Space* (Lincoln, Nebr.: University of Nebraska Press, 1993), p. 118.

9. William D. Marbach, "A Special Breed, a Lust to Soar," *Newsweek*, February 10, 1986, p. 29.

Chapter 2

1. Robert T. Hohler, *"I Touch the Future . . .": The Story of Christa McAuliffe* (New York: Random House, 1986), p. 29.

2. Katherine Barrett and Richard Greene, "The People Behind the Headlines," *Ladies' Home Journal*, December 1985, pp. 34, 36.

3. Hohler, p. 8.

4. Barrett and Greene, p. 36.

5. Hohler, p. 52.

6. Ron Arias, "A Lesson in Uncommon Valor," *People*, February 10, 1986, p. 36.

Chapter 3

1. Grace George Corrigan, *A Journal for Christa: Christa McAuliffe, Teacher in Space* (Lincoln, Nebr.: University of Nebraska Press, 1993), p. 97.

2. Ibid., p. 98.

3. Ibid., p. 85.

4. David Friend, "A Teacher Crams for a Classroom in Orbit," *Life*, December 1985, p. 36.

5. Robert T. Hohler, *"I Touch the Future . . .": The Story of Christa McAuliffe* (New York: Random House, 1986), p. 125.

6. David H. Van Biema, "Christa McAuliffe Gets NASA's Nod to Conduct America's First Classroom in Space," *People*, August 5, 1985, p. 28.

7. Katherine Barrett and Richard Greene, "The People Behind the Headlines," *Ladies' Home Journal*, December 1985, p. 36.

8. Van Biema, p. 35.

9. Friend, p. 36.

Chapter 4

1. William D. Marbach, "A Special Breed, a Lust to Soar," *Newsweek*, February 10, 1986, p. 29.

2. "The Space Teacher," *Life*, March 1986, p. 8.

3. David Friend, "A Teacher Crams for a Classroom in Orbit," *Life*, December 1985, p. 38.

4. Ibid., p. 40.

5. Katherine Barrett and Richard Greene, "The People Behind the Headlines," *Ladies' Home Journal*, December 1985, p. 36.

6. Friend, p. 40.

7. Barrett and Greene, p. 34.

8. David H. Van Biema, "Christa McAuliffe Gets NASA's Nod to Conduct America's First Classroom in Space," *People*, August 5, 1985, p. 35.

9. Michael D. Cole, *Challenger: America's Space Tragedy* (Springfield, N.J.: Enslow Publishers, Inc., 1995), p. 30.

10. Timothy Levi Biel, *The Challenger* (San Diego: Lucent Books, 1991), p. 40.

11. Kathryn Casey, "Remembering the Challenger," *Ladies' Home Journal*, January 1996, p. 149.

12. Marbach, p. 29.

Chapter 5

1. William D. Marbach, "'One Cruel Moment' While the Children Looked On," *Newsweek*, February 10, 1986, p. 30.

2. Mike Pride, "'There Had Been a Death in the Family,'" *Newsweek*, February 10, 1986, p. 42.

3. Barbara Embury, *The Dream Is Alive: A Flight of Discovery Aboard the Space Shuttle* (New York: Harper & Row Publishers, 1990), p. 10.

4. William J. Cook, "Shuttling Cautiously Ahead, 10 Years Later," *U.S. News & World Report*, January 29, 1996, p. 11.

5. Kathryn Casey, "Remembering the Challenger," *Ladies' Home Journal*, January 1996, p. 151.

6. Ed Magnuson, "Fixing NASA," *Time*, June 9, 1986, p. 20.

7. Geoffrey Cowley, "Special Report," *Newsweek*, October 10, 1988, p. 27.

8. Cynthia Hanson, "Survivor: A Life Relaunched," *Good Housekeeping*, January 1996, p. 26.

9. Casey, p. 101.

10. Grace Corrigan, as told to Donna Elizabeth Boetig, "The Whole World Loved My Daughter," *McCall's*, January 1996, p. 65.

GLOSSARY

Discovery—The shuttle that was built after the space shuttle *Challenger* exploded.

Enterprise—America's first test space shuttle.

external fuel tank—A huge aluminum tank that is attached to the underside of the shuttle and filled with liquid hydrogen and oxygen to fuel the orbiter's three main engines during launch.

NASA—National Aeronautics and Space Administration, created in 1958 to lead America's exploration into space.

O-ring—A rubber pressure seal located on the solid rocket boosters to prevent gases from escaping.

Rogers Commission—The thirteen-member panel called together by President Ronald Reagan to investigate the *Challenger* explosion.

solid rocket booster—The two rockets attached to opposite sides of the external fuel tank. They provide additional power for liftoff.

space shuttle—The first reusable spacecraft. It is made up of three main parts: the external fuel tank, the orbiter, and the solid rocket boosters.

FURTHER READING

Biel, Timothy Levi. *The Challenger.* San Diego: Lucent Books, 1991.

Billings, Charlene W. *Christa McAuliffe: Pioneer Space Teacher.* Hillside, N.J.: Enslow Publishers, Inc., 1986.

Cassutt, Michael. *Who's Who in Space.* New York: Macmillan Publishing Co., 1993.

Cole, Michael D. *Challenger: America's Space Tragedy.* Springfield, N.J.: Enslow Publishers, Inc., 1995.

Corrigan, Grace George. *A Journal for Christa: Christa McAuliffe, Teacher in Space.* Lincoln, Nebr.: University of Nebraska Press, 1993.

Embury, Barbara. *The Dream Is Alive: A Flight of Discovery Aboard the Space Shuttle.* New York: Harper Collins Children's Books, 1990.

Hohler, Robert T. *"I Touch the Future . . .": The Story of Christa McAuliffe.* New York: Random House, 1986.

McAleer, Neil. *The Omni Space Almanac.* Mahwah, N.J.: World Almanac, 1987.

INDEX